I0618422

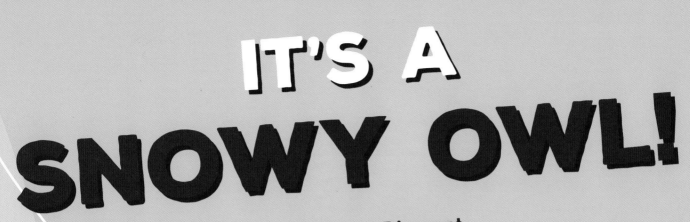

IT'S A SNOWY OWL!

by Kerry Dinmont

BUMBA BOOKS™

LERNER PUBLICATIONS ◆ MINNEAPOLIS

Note to Educators:

Throughout this book, you'll find critical thinking questions. These can be used to engage young readers in thinking critically about the topic and in using the text and photos to do so.

Lerner Publications Company
A division of Lerner Publishing Group, Inc.
241 First Avenue North
Minneapolis, MN 55401 USA

For reading levels and more information, look up this title at www.lernerbooks.com.

Library of Congress Cataloging-in-Publication Data

Names: Dinmont, Kerry, 1982– author.
Title: It's a snowy owl! / Kerry Dinmont.
Other titles: It is a snowy owl
Description: Minneapolis : Lerner Publications, [2018] | Series: Bumba books. Polar animals | Audience: Ages 4–7. | Audience: K to grade 3. | Includes bibliographical references and index.
Identifiers: LCCN 2018006011 (print) | LCCN 2017060879 (ebook) | ISBN 9781512482898 (eb pdf) | ISBN 9781512482799 (lb : alk. paper) | ISBN 9781541526976 (pb : alk. paper)
Subjects: LCSH: Snowy owl—Juvenile literature. | Owls—Polar regions—Juvenile literature. | Birds—Polar regions—Juvenile literature.
Classification: LCC QL696.S83 (print) | LCC QL696.S83 D56 2018 (ebook) | DDC 598.9/7—dc23

LC record available at https://lccn.loc.gov/2018006011

Manufactured in the United States of America
1 – CG – 7/15/18

Table of
Contents

Snowy Owls Fly

Snowy owls are birds.

They live in northern North America.

Adult males are mostly white. Females are white and black. White feathers help them hide in the snow.

Why do you think snowy owls need to hide?

7

Feathers keep snowy owls warm.

They have feathers on their feet

and legs too.

Snowy owls live far north

in the summer.

They follow their food in the winter.

Snowy owls eat small mammals

and birds.

They often eat lemmings.

lemming

Snowy owls hunt day
and night.

They listen and watch

for prey.

They catch prey

with their talons.

Females lay three to eleven eggs.

Chicks hatch a few weeks later.

The male hunts for food.

The female feeds the food

to the chicks.

Chicks can fly by seven weeks old.

Why do you think the male hunts for food?

Male owls hoot to protect

their nests.

They protect their

hunting grounds.

Parts of a Snowy Owl

feathers

beak

talons

Picture Glossary

chicks

baby birds

mammals

animals that give birth to live young and feed them milk

prey

animals hunted as food

talons

claws at the end of an owl's feet

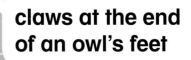

Read More

Alinsky, Shelby. *Hoot, Owl!* Washington, DC: National Geographic, 2015.

Boothroyd, Jennifer. *From Egg to Owl*. Minneapolis: Lerner Publications, 2017.

Marsh, Laura. *Owls*. Washington, DC: National Geographic, 2014.

Index

Photo Credits

The images in this book are used with the permission of: © sarkophoto/iStock.com, pp. 4–5; © karl umbriaco/Shutterstock.com, pp. 6, 23 (top right); © Josef Pittner/Shutterstock.com, pp. 8–9; © Dmitri Gomon/Shutterstock.com, p. 10; © Sergey Krasnoshchokov/Shutterstock.com, p. 13; © longtaildog/Shutterstock.com, pp. 14–15; © Lillian Tveit/Shutterstock.com, pp. 16–17, 23 (top left); © merlinpf/iStock.com, p. 18; © Indigo Images/Shutterstock.com, p. 21; © Iakov Filimonov/Shutterstock.com, p. 22; © Holly Kuchera/Shutterstock.com, p. 23 (bottom right); © Ester Sall/Shutterstock.com, p. 23 (bottom left).

Front Cover: © Sergey Krasnoshchokov/Shutterstock.com.